Listening Breakthrough for the TOEIC®Test

TOEIC®テストのリスニング攻略

Terry O'Brien
Kei Mihara
Sakujiro Shuno
Hiroshi Kimura

NAN'UN-DO

Listening Breakthrough for the TOEIC®Test

Copyright © 2015

Terry O'Brien
Kei Mihara
Sakujiro Shuno
Hiroshi Kimura

All rights Reserved

No part of this book may be reproduced in any form without written permission from the authors and Nan'un-do Co., Ltd.

このテキストの音声を無料で視聴（ストリーミング）・ダウンロードできます。自習用音声としてご活用ください。
以下のサイトにアクセスしてテキスト番号で検索してください。

https://nanun-do.com　テキスト番号 [511630]

※ 無線 LAN（WiFi）に接続してのご利用を推奨いたします。

※ 音声ダウンロードは Zip ファイルでの提供になります。
　お使いの機器によっては別途ソフトウェア（アプリケーション）の導入が必要となります。

※ Listening Breakthrough for the TOEIC Test 音声ダウンロードページは以下の QR コードからもご利用になれます。

はじめに

　Listening Breakthrough for the TOEIC®Test は、TOEIC® テスト対策の一環として、リスニングを集中して学習するために作成したテキストです。日常の身近なテーマやビジネスシーンでよく見られる場面や表現で効率よく学習し、リスニング力を向上させることを目指しています。

　急速にグローバル化が進む中、国際社会で活躍できる英語コミュニケーション能力のある人材を育成することが求められています。そのため TOEIC® テストが個人による受験のほかに、多くの大学・企業・団体等で活用されています。大学では TOEIC® スコアで単位認定をしたり、TOEIC® テストの受験対策講座を提供しているところもあります。また、企業では社員の海外出張の基準や昇進・昇格の要件として利用しています。

　本書は、TOEIC® テストのリスニングセクションを攻略し、リスニング力が確実に身につくように、次の6つの特徴があります。

1. TOEIC® 頻出トピックを「日常生活」と「ビジネス」に分けることで、分野ごとに集中して効率よく学習ができます。
2. Warm-up では、各トピックに関連する TOEIC® 頻出語句や頻出表現が確認できます。
3. Test Questions では、実際の TOEIC® テスト（Part 1 ～ Part 4）にチャレンジできます。
4. 5つのユニットが終わるごとに、Mini Test にチャレンジできます。
5. Follow-up では、リスニング攻略に必要なコツがつかめます。
6. 各ユニットの Script Dictation でリスニングチェックができます。

　TOEIC® テストで高得点のカギを握るのはリスニング力です。短期間で TOEIC® スコアをアップする方法は、リスニングを集中的に学習し、リスニング問題のスピードに慣れ、集中力を持続させることにあります。リスニング力の強化は、TOEIC® スコアアップのために乗り越えなくてはならない壁なのです。本書を通して、リスニングのためのストラテジーを身につけ、リスニング力を向上させ、実際の TOEIC® テストで目標とするスコアを取得されることを願っています。

2015 年春
著者

本書の使い方

　本書は全 24 ユニットで、前半の 12 ユニットは日常生活に関するトピック、後半の 12 ユニットはビジネスに関するトピックです。各ユニットは Warm-up と Test Questions で構成しています。Warm-up では各ユニットのテーマに即した頻出語彙や表現などの確認をします。Test Questions では実際の TOEIC® 形式の問題にチャレンジします。また、5 つのユニットが終わるごとに Mini Test があります。

Warm-up

Check 1　TOEIC® リスニング頻出語彙の意味をチェックしてください。
Check 2　TOEIC® リスニング頻出表現などをチェックしてください。

Test Questions

Part 1　Photographs

1 枚の写真について 4 つの短い説明文を聞き、最も適切に描写をしているものを (A) 〜 (D) から 1 つ選んでください。

Part 2　Question-Response

1 つの質問または文と、それに対する 3 つの応答を聞き、最も適切なものを (A) 〜 (C) から 1 つ選んでください。

Part 3　Short Conversations

2 人の会話を聞き、設問を聞いたあと、その設問に対する最も適切な答えを (A) 〜 (D) から 1 つ選んでください。1 つの会話に設問が 3 つあります。

Part 4　Short Talks

1 人が話すミニトークを聞き、設問を聞いたあと、その設問に対する最も適切な答えを (A) 〜 (D) から 1 つ選んでください。1 つのミニトークに設問が 3 つあります。

Follow-up

TOEIC® テストのリスニング攻略のミニ情報です。

TOEIC® について

- TOEIC® とは Test of English for International Communication の略称で、英語によるコミュニケーション能力を評価するためのテストです。

- 出題形式は、リスニング（45分間、Part 1 ～ Part 4、全100問）とリーディング（75分間、Part 5 ～ Part 7、全100問）から成り、マークシート方式です。

- テスト結果は、リスニングセクション（5点～495点、5点刻み）、リーディングセクション（5点～495点、5点刻み）でトータル（10点～990点、5点刻み）のスコアで評価されます。

- TOEIC® テストは、単語やスペリングはアメリカ英語です。

1. リスニングセクションの問題（45分、100問）

Part 1	Photographs（写真描写問題）	10問	1枚の写真について4つの短い説明文が1度だけ放送される。説明文は印刷されていない。4つのうち、写真を最も的確に描写しているものを選び解答用紙にマークする。
Part 2	Question-Response（応答問題）	30問	1つの質問または文章とそれに対する3つの答えがそれぞれ1度だけ放送される。印刷はされていない。設問に対して最もふさわしい答えを選び解答用紙にマークする。
Part 3	Short Conversations（会話問題）	30問	2人の人物による会話が1度だけ放送される。印刷はされていない。会話を聞いて問題用紙に印刷された設問（設問は放送される）と解答を読み、4つの答えの中から最も適当なものを選び解答用紙にマークする。各会話には設問が3問ずつある。
Part 4	Short Talks（説明文問題）	30問	アナウンスやナレーションのようなミニトークが1度だけ放送される。印刷はされていない。各トークを聞いて問題用紙に印刷された設問（設問は放送される）と解答を読み、4つの答えの中から最も適当なものを選び解答用紙にマークする。各トークには質問が3問ずつある。

2. アメリカ英語とイギリス英語の発音

- アメリカ英語の他に、イギリス英語、カナダ英語、オーストラリア（ニュージーランドを含む）英語で、それぞれ25％の割合で発音されますので、4か国語の発音に慣れることが必要です。

- カナダ英語はほとんどアメリカ英語と同じで、オーストラリア英語はイギリス英語とほぼ同じ発音を共有しています。したがって、アメリカ英語とイギリス英語の発音の違いを理解すれば、カナダ英語とオーストラリア英語も聞き取れるようになります。

[example]

	car	can't	castle
アメリカ英語	[kɑ:r]「カァー」	[kæn(t)]「キャン(ト)」	[kǽsl]「キャッスル」
イギリス英語	[kɑ:]「カー」	[kɑ:nt]「カーン(ト)」	[kɑ́:sl]「カースル」

Contents

Everyday Life：日常生活のトピック

Unit 1   **Fashion and Shopping**（ファッションとショッピング）   8
服の試着 / プレゼントの購入

Unit 2   **Eating Out**（外食）   10
料理の注文 / レストランのオープン

Unit 3   **Entertainment**（娯楽）   12
映画のチケットを購入 / 公演前にすること

Unit 4   **Housing and Family Life**（住まいと家庭生活）   14
部屋の掃除 / 家のリフォーム

Unit 5   **Media**（メディア）   16
映画の配役 / 公平な報道

Unit 6   **Mini Test 1**   18

Unit 7   **Travel and Airports**（旅行と空港）   20
入国審査官の質問 / 機内放送

Unit 8   **Hotels**（ホテル）   22
宿泊の手続き / ホテル経営

Unit 9   **The Weather**（天気）   24
テレビの天気予報 / 1週間の天気

Unit 10   **Education**（教育）   26
仕事につながる大学教育 / 授業中の学生

Unit 11   **Fitness**（フィットネス）   28
フィットネスクラブへ行く理由 / スポーツをする利点

Unit 12   **Mini Test 2**   30

Business：ビジネスのトピック

Unit 13 **Business Trips**（出張) ... 32
ホテルをチェックアウト / 領収書をもらう

Unit 14 **Production and Sales**（生産と販売) ... 34
広告で伸びる売上高 / 薄利で大量販売

Unit 15 **Job Hunting and Recruitment**（就活と社員募集) ... 36
面接 / 秘書の求人

Unit 16 **Accounting**（会計) ... 38
間違いのない会計 / 会計学を学ぶための学校

Unit 17 **Personnel**（人事) ... 40
職場での迷惑な私語 / グループを作らず仲良く

Unit 18 **Mini Test 3** ... 42

Unit 19 **Customer Service**（カスタマーサービス) ... 44
商品の遅配に対応 / テキパキした発送作業

Unit 20 **Order and Shipping**（注文と輸送) ... 46
注文品を大量発送 / 能率と信頼

Unit 21 **Negotiations**（交渉) ... 48
遅延の解決 / 積極的な制裁

Unit 22 **Presentations**（プレゼン) ... 50
発表者に質問 / スクリーンを使った説明

Unit 23 **Marketing**（マーケティング) ... 52
売上下落の理由 / 社員のスケジュール調整

Unit 24 **Mini Test 4** ... 54

7

Unit 1 Fashion and Shopping

Warm-up

Check 1 Where can you buy these things? Put the words in the appropriate boxes.

| ballpoint pen | envelope | fridge | greeting card | jacket | pants |
| printer | shirt | stapler | sweater | vacuum cleaner | washing machine |

Apparel Store	Electronics Store	Stationery Store

Check 2 Match the questions or comments (1-5) with the correct responses (a-e). Write the letters on the lines.

1. Is it the right size? _____
2. Do you have your receipt? _____
3. I'm looking for a sleeveless dress. _____
4. Can I try on this long skirt? _____
5. Would you like a replacement? _____

a. Yes, here it is.
b. Well, I'd rather have my money back.
c. Certainly. The fitting rooms are over there.
d. No, it isn't. It's too small.
e. What about this one? It's $90.

Test Questions

Part 1 Photographs   2

1.   Ⓐ Ⓑ Ⓒ Ⓓ

2.   Ⓐ Ⓑ Ⓒ Ⓓ

Part 2 Question-Response   3

3. Mark your answer.   Ⓐ Ⓑ Ⓒ
4. Mark your answer.   Ⓐ Ⓑ Ⓒ

Part 3 Short Conversations   4

5. Why is the man buying Jill a present?
   (A) Christmas is coming soon.   (B) He forgot to buy her a present last year.
   (C) It's her birthday.   (D) She asked him to.

6. How does the man feel about a watch for Jill?
   (A) It is too expensive.   (B) It will be the perfect gift.
   (C) Jill already has one.   (D) He would rather give her something to wear.

7. What does the woman finally suggest?
   (A) A hat and gloves set   (B) Waiting until Jill's next birthday
   (C) A wristwatch   (D) Something to wear

Part 4 Short Talks   5

8. What did the man go shopping for?
   (A) All day yesterday   (B) To buy himself a new suit
   (C) He enjoys shopping.   (D) To buy his girlfriend a present

9. What problem did the man have?
   (A) He wasn't able to find a present at all.
   (B) He didn't know his girlfriend's shoes and clothes sizes.
   (C) He didn't have much time.
   (D) The shops were closed.

10. What was the man's final decision?
    (A) To ask Jill what she wanted (B) To go to another store
    (C) To give Jill a pen   (D) To go shopping again today

Follow-up

[t] の音変化

- **Part 4** に tried to find a（見つけようとした）「チュライトファインダ」という音声が聞こえます。英語は単語が1つひとつ発音されるのではなく、いくつかの単語がまとまって発音され、音の連結〔つながること〕で音変化が起こります。
- Let's try it!（やってみよう！）は「レッチュライ(ト)」と聞こえます。try（試みる）の [t] は「チュ」のように聞こえることがあります。
- [t] 音は、party（パーティ）は「パーリー」、I got it.（わかった）は「アイガリ」と聞こえることがあります。

Unit 2 Eating Out

Warm-up

Check 1 To what category do these things belong? Put the words in the appropriate boxes.

> beer   bitter   coke   juice   noodles   omelet
> salty   spaghetti   spicy   soda   steak   sweet

Beverages	Dishes	Flavors

Check 2 Match the questions (1-5) with the correct responses (a-e). Write the letters on the lines.

1. Excuse me. Are you ready to order? _____
2. What would you like to drink? _____
3. Would you like to go out to dinner? _____
4. How would you like your coffee? _____
5. Could you pass the salt, please? _____

a. Black, no sugar, please.
b. Well, I'd love to, but I can't today.
c. Yes. I'd like a steak, please.
d. Sure, here you are.
e. Just water for me.

Test Questions

Part 1 Photographs   6

1.

Ⓐ Ⓑ Ⓒ Ⓓ

2.

Ⓐ Ⓑ Ⓒ Ⓓ

10

Part 2 Question-Response 7

3. Mark your answer. Ⓐ Ⓑ Ⓒ
4. Mark your answer. Ⓐ Ⓑ Ⓒ

Part 3 Short Conversations 8

5. What are the man and woman doing?
    (A) Leaving a restaurant
    (B) Deciding what to have for dinner
    (C) Discussing the desserts
    (D) Having dinner at home

6. What is similar about the man and woman?
    (A) They are both full.
    (B) They both want coffee.
    (C) Neither can decide what cake to order.
    (D) They both want cake and a drink.

7. What is the woman going to order?
    (A) A piece of chocolate cake
    (B) Cake and coffee
    (C) Cake and tea
    (D) Just tea

Part 4 Short Talks 9

8. What is the article about?
    (A) A new coffee shop
    (B) A new restaurant
    (C) The station kiosk
    (D) A convenience store's opening

9. Why does the business have a chance to be successful?
    (A) Because it is new.
    (B) Because it is in a good location, and has a variety of lunches.
    (C) Because it is in an out-of-the-way place.
    (D) Because it is too far from the station.

10. What do we know about the speaker?
    (A) She lives near the station.
    (B) She is in a hurry.
    (C) She would like to eat with a friend.
    (D) She wants to eat by herself.

Follow-up

音の強弱

- **Part 4** に about a restaurant（レストランについて）「(ァ)バウタ・レストラン（ト）」があります。単語はアクセント（強勢）の部分は強く発音され、アクセントのない部分は弱く発音されます。
- 前置詞 about も「(ァ)バウ(ト)」のようにアクセントのある「バウ」以外は、弱く発音します。
- Think about it!（そのことを考えてください！）は「スィンカバウティ(ト)」と聞こえます。「バウ」が強い音で聞こえますが、これは about「(ァ)バウ(ト)」の音です。
- 文の場合、意味的に重要な部分は強く、重要でない部分は弱く発音されます。

Unit 3 Entertainment

Warm-up

Check 1 To what category do these things belong? Put the words in the appropriate boxes.

| actor | aisle | audience | cast | drawing | knitting |
| magician | pottery | row | screen | sculpture | stage |

Inside the Theater	Arts and Crafts	People

Check 2 Choose the correct word from the box to complete each sentence.

| astonished | conductor | expensive | perform | plot |

1. This movie was disappointing. The scenes were good but the (   ) was confusing.
2. Successful hit movies are very (   ) to make.
3. This is a really great movie. I saw it yesterday and was (   ) by the special effects.
4. The music was wonderful, and the (   ) led the orchestra very well.
5. Kate is a folk dancer, and she loves to (   ) at special events.

Test Questions

Part 1 Photographs   10

1.   Ⓐ Ⓑ Ⓒ Ⓓ

2.   Ⓐ Ⓑ Ⓒ Ⓓ

Part 2 Question-Response 🔊 11

3. Mark your answer. Ⓐ Ⓑ Ⓒ
4. Mark your answer. Ⓐ Ⓑ Ⓒ

Part 3 Short Conversations 🔊 12

5. When does the movie start?
   (A) At six
   (B) At seven forty-five
   (C) At a quarter past eight
   (D) Just before eight

6. How many people are in the woman's group?
   (A) Four
   (B) Two children and two adults
   (C) Three and the woman
   (D) Three including the woman

7. What is the woman probably going to do after buying tickets?
   (A) Go straight home
   (B) Go shopping
   (C) Have pizza at Wally's
   (D) Watch another movie

Part 4 Short Talks 🔊 13

8. What is the audience requested to do prior to the performance?
   (A) Applaud politely
   (B) Read the program carefully
   (C) Stop smoking
   (D) Switch off their phones

9. How many times will the violinist perform this program?
   (A) Each day this week
   (B) Only today
   (C) As many as necessary
   (D) About an hour and a half

10. What can the audience do during the break?
    (A) Eat and drink something in the lobby
    (B) Have dinner at the restaurant next door
    (C) Meet the violinist in person
    (D) There's not enough time to do anything.

Follow-up

[l] の音変化

- **Part 3** に one adult (ワナダゥト), children (チゥドレン), called (コーゥド) が出てきます。それぞれ [l] 音の「ゥ」は舌先を上の歯茎の裏にくっつけ「ゥ」と発音します。そしてそのまま次の「ト/ド」につなげて発音します。
- Control yourself. (ほどほどにね) は「コンチュロゥユアセゥフ」と聞こえます。[l] 音は、後ろに母音が来るときは land「ランド」のように「ラ」音に聞こえますが、それ以外は「ゥ」音に聞こえます。

Unit 4 Housing and Family Life

Warm-up

Check 1 To what category do these things belong? Put the words in the appropriate boxes.

| apartment | bed making | block | cleaning | condo | dormitory |
| downtown | gardening | house | neighborhood | suburbs | washing |

Living Spaces	Household Chores	Areas

Check 2 Choose the correct word from the box to complete each sentence.

| outskirts | residents | sale | spacious | stairs |

1. Emily has a (　　　　) living room, so she is buying a large sofa.
2. The (　　　　) of this apartment building are friendly, and they're quiet, too.
3. The elevator isn't working now, so we have to take the (　　　　) to the fifth floor.
4. There are nice apartments for (　　　　) near the beach.
5. I love nature, so I want to live in the (　　　　).

Test Questions

Part 1 Photographs　　　14

1. 　　Ⓐ Ⓑ Ⓒ Ⓓ

2. 　　Ⓐ Ⓑ Ⓒ Ⓓ

Part 2 Question-Response　　　　　　　　　　　　　　🔵 15

3. Mark your answer.　　　　　　　　　　　　　Ⓐ　Ⓑ　Ⓒ
4. Mark your answer.　　　　　　　　　　　　　Ⓐ　Ⓑ　Ⓒ

Part 3 Short Conversations　　　　　　　　　　　　🔵 16

5. What is wrong with the man's room?
   - (A) It is a mess.
   - (B) It smells bad.
   - (C) It's too small.
   - (D) It's too dark.

6. Why does the man say he can't clean his room now?
   - (A) Peter is coming over.
   - (B) It looks terrible.
   - (C) He wants to play catch.
   - (D) He's studying.

7. How much time does the woman give the man to clean the room?
   - (A) A week
   - (B) A whole day
   - (C) When he gets home
   - (D) Right now

Part 4 Short Talks　　　　　　　　　　　　　　　🔵 17

8. What is the man's job?
   - (A) He cleans houses.
   - (B) He is a carpenter.
   - (C) He sells home insurance.
   - (D) He sells real estate.

9. What will the man do with the kitchen?
   - (A) He is going to change the location.
   - (B) He is going to make it bigger.
   - (C) He will put in a window and a new door.
   - (D) He will turn it into a dining area.

10. What does the man say the house will look like when he's finished?
    - (A) Much more colorful
    - (B) Much more comfortable
    - (C) Much more convenient
    - (D) Like a new house

Follow-up

語尾の [t] 音

- **Part 3** に「ラィナゥ」「オーラィ」「ドゥィットモロゥ」といった音声が聞こえます。それぞれ right now (今すぐ)、all right (よろしい)、do it tomorrow (それを明日しなさい) です。語尾の [t] 音は破裂せず、音として聞こえないことがあります。
- Take care of it. (気をつけて)「ティケアラヴィ(ト)」は、文尾の [t] 音が聞こえないことがよくあります。単語の最後に来る破裂音 [t, d, p, b, k, g] は音が消失する傾向があります。

Unit 5 Media

Warm-up

Check 1 Match the words to the definitions. Write the letters on the lines.

1. source   _____   a. person who reports the news on TV
2. editor   _____   b. person who writes about the news
3. media   _____   c. someone who gives a reporter information
4. newscaster   _____   d. person who chooses the articles that will be printed
5. journalist   _____   e. newspapers, TV, radio, the Internet, and so on

Check 2 Choose the correct word from the box to complete each sentence.

| commentary | medium | print | publication | purchase |

1. A newspaper is a written (   ) containing news, information, and advertising.
2. A blog is a website where a person can air his or her (   ).
3. Advertising is a form of communication that persuades customers to (   ) a product.
4. Television is a communication (   ) for transmitting and receiving moving images.
5. News is information broadcast over the radio or television, presented online, or published in (   ) media.

Test Questions

Part 1 Photographs   18

1.

Ⓐ Ⓑ Ⓒ Ⓓ

2.

Ⓐ Ⓑ Ⓒ Ⓓ

Part 2 Question-Response 🎧 19

3. Mark your answer. Ⓐ Ⓑ Ⓒ
4. Mark your answer. Ⓐ Ⓑ Ⓒ

Part 3 Short Conversations 🎧 20

5. What does the man want to know about the woman?
   (A) About her next movie
   (B) What part she plays in the movie
   (C) If she enjoys playing the queen
   (D) If she has a strong character

6. When were the reviews written?
   (A) Before the movie came out
   (B) During the filming
   (C) This morning
   (D) After the movie was first shown

7. Why was the woman excited?
   (A) Reviewers praised her performance.
   (B) She met the queen in person.
   (C) Opening night was bad.
   (D) The reviews were not that good.

Part 4 Short Talks 🎧 21

8. How does the speaker feel?
   (A) Pleased
   (B) Surprised
   (C) Enthusiastic
   (D) Disappointed

9. What kind of reporting does the speaker say newspapers should do?
   (A) Aggressive
   (B) Biased
   (C) Objective
   (D) Cruel

10. What does the speaker say might be the result of the media's current style of reporting?
    (A) Fairer news coverage
    (B) The government's inability to function
    (C) A quick economic recovery
    (D) A better government

Follow-up

音の連結〔子音＋母音〕

- **Part 1** の One of the men（男性の1人は）は「ワノブザメン」と聞こえます。one of は「ワンオブ」ではなく「ワノブ」と発音します。one [wʌn] の語尾の [n] 音と、of [əv] の語頭の [ə]〔母音〕が連結して音声変化が起こり、「ワノブ」となります。
- Get along together!（仲良くしましょう）は「ゲッタロン(グ)トゲザー」と聞こえます。along の語頭の母音 [ə] は、直前の語尾の子音 [t] とつながって発音されます。

Unit 6　Mini Test 1

Part 1　Photographs　　　　　　　　　　　　　　　　　　🔘 22

1. Ⓐ Ⓑ Ⓒ Ⓓ

2. Ⓐ Ⓑ Ⓒ Ⓓ

3. Ⓐ Ⓑ Ⓒ Ⓓ

4. Ⓐ Ⓑ Ⓒ Ⓓ

Part 2　Question-Response　　　　　　　　　　　　　　　🔘 23

5. Mark your answer.　　　　　　　　　　　　　Ⓐ Ⓑ Ⓒ

6. Mark your answer.　　　　　　　　　　　　　Ⓐ Ⓑ Ⓒ

7. Mark your answer.　　　　　　　　　　　　　Ⓐ Ⓑ Ⓒ

8. Mark your answer.　　　　　　　　　　　　　Ⓐ Ⓑ Ⓒ

9. Mark your answer.　　　　　　　　　　　　　Ⓐ Ⓑ Ⓒ

Part 3 Short Conversations 24

10. What was the man's problem this morning?
    (A) He lost his ticket.
    (B) He missed his train.
    (C) The trains were not running on time.
    (D) The station was crowded.

11. What time did the express leave?
    (A) It departed at 7:30.
    (B) It was cancelled.
    (C) It left at 7:40.
    (D) It was half an hour behind schedule.

12. How did the woman come to the office?
    (A) She got a taxi.
    (B) She took the bus.
    (C) She walked.
    (D) She didn't say.

Part 4 Short Talks 25

13. How did the man learn about the car?
    (A) He saw an ad in the paper.
    (B) He saw one in the street.
    (C) He saw it as he walked by the showroom.
    (D) A commercial on TV caught his eye.

14. What would make the car a little more expensive?
    (A) The four-door model
    (B) The air conditioner
    (C) The GPS system
    (D) The stereo system

15. Why is it going to take such a long time for the man to get his car?
    (A) A lot of people have already ordered it.
    (B) He forgot to put his name down for it.
    (C) He ordered so many optional items.
    (D) He hasn't decided if he wants to buy one yet.

Unit 7   Travel and Airports

Warm-up

Check 1   Where can you see or hear about these things? Put the words in the appropriate boxes.

> airfare   aisle seat   baggage claim   boarding gate
> check-in   fasten seatbelt sign   flight attendant   guided tour
> Immigration and Customs   itinerary   tourist attraction   upright position

At the Airport	In an Airplane	At a Travel Agency

Check 2   Match the questions (1-5) with the responses (a-e). Write the letters on the lines.

1. May I see your boarding pass and passport, please?   _____
2. How was your canoeing trip?   _____
3. How many bags are you checking?   _____
4. Are you looking forward to your trip?   _____
5. Where do you usually go on holidays?   _____

a. Yes, I can't wait.
b. To the beach in California.
c. Certainly. Here you are.
d. Just this one.
e. I almost fell in the water.

Test Questions

Part 1   Photographs   26

1. Ⓐ Ⓑ Ⓒ Ⓓ

2. Ⓐ Ⓑ Ⓒ Ⓓ

Part 2 Question-Response　　27

3. Mark your answer.　　Ⓐ Ⓑ Ⓒ
4. Mark your answer.　　Ⓐ Ⓑ Ⓒ

Part 3 Short Conversations　　28

5. When will the woman return to her country?
   (A) In two weeks　　(B) In ten days
   (C) Next week　　(D) The day after tomorrow

6. What is the purpose of the woman's visit?
   (A) She is here on business.　　(B) She is on a holiday.
   (C) She is visiting friends.　　(D) She wants to live here permanently.

7. Why is the woman using three hotels?
   (A) She doesn't like to stay in the same place.
   (B) She likes living in hotels.
   (C) She can't make up his mind.
   (D) She is traveling to several cities.

Part 4 Short Talks　　29

8. Who is talking?
   (A) A cabin attendant　　(B) A member of ground crew
   (C) The bus driver　　(D) The captain of the plane

9. What is mentioned about the flight?
   (A) How long it will take　　(B) The departure time
   (C) The meal service　　(D) The route to be taken

10. What is mentioned about the destination?
    (A) The weather upon arrival　　(B) The name of the airport
    (C) The arrival gate number　　(D) Where to have a good time

Follow-up

写真問題攻略のコツ (1)

- Part 1 の at the check-in counter（チェックインカウンターで）は「アッザチェキンカウンタ」と聞こえます。at は次の単語が子音で始まると、語尾の [t] 音が消失して「アッ」と聞こえます。
- at the ...「アッザ」という音声変化は、at the station, at the hotel など、頻繁に使われるので、耳を慣らしておきましょう。
- 写真問題では、物が写っている場合は、物と物との位置関係に注目しましょう。写真問題攻略のコツは at, in, on, under, between, from, behind といった前置詞を聞き取ることです。

Unit 8　Hotels

Warm-up

Check 1   Match the words to the definitions. Write the letters on the lines.

1. concierge _____
2. reserve _____
3. twin room _____
4. housekeeper _____
5. porter _____

a. person responsible for cleaning hotel rooms
b. staff member of a hotel who assists guests
c. to arrange for a room in a hotel
d. room with two beds
e. hotel attendant who carries travelers' bags

Check 2   Match questions or comments (1-5) with the responses (a-e). Write the letters on the lines.

1. I'd like to reserve a room for tomorrow night. _____
2. Here's my credit card. _____
3. I'd like to make a dinner reservation. _____
4. Did you have anything from the minibar? _____
5. There is something wrong with the airconditioning. _____

a. Yes, I had one bottle of beer.
b. I'll send someone to fix it.
c. I'm sorry, but we're fully booked.
d. I'll put you through to the restaurant.
e. Could you enter your PIN, please?

Test Questions

Part 1   Photographs　　　30

1.　　Ⓐ Ⓑ Ⓒ Ⓓ

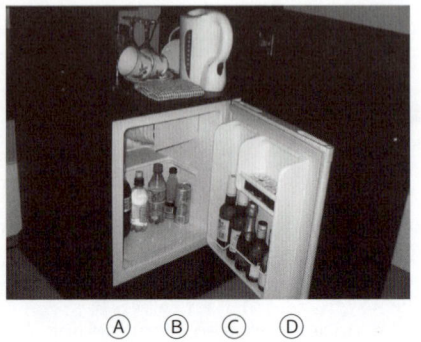

2.　　Ⓐ Ⓑ Ⓒ Ⓓ

Part 2 Question-Response   🔊 31

3. Mark your answer.   Ⓐ Ⓑ Ⓒ
4. Mark your answer.   Ⓐ Ⓑ Ⓒ

Part 3 Short Conversations   🔊 32

5. How long is the man staying?
   (A) Two nights   (B) He is leaving on Friday.
   (C) He's not sure.   (D) Overnight

6. How did the man reserve his room?
   (A) By phone   (B) His secretary did it.
   (C) On the Internet   (D) In person

7. What does the room 702 have?
   (A) A desk and chair   (B) Two beds
   (C) A minibar   (D) Internet access

Part 4 Short Talks   🔊 33

8. When did the hotel open for business?
   (A) All these years   (B) 100 years ago
   (C) In 2000   (D) In 30 different cities

9. What does the ad say the hotel's key to success is?
   (A) A low price but good service   (B) Friendly staff
   (C) Many locations   (D) Comfortable rooms

10. What does the hotel offer business guests?
    (A) Free meal   (B) Extra bed
    (C) Cheaper rates   (D) Larger room

Follow-up

会話問題攻略のコツ (1)

- **Part 3** の Could I have your name?（お名前をいただけますか）は「クッダイ(ア)ヴユアネィ(ム)」と聞こえます。会話特有の許可・依頼・提案の表現に慣れることが大切です。Could I ...?（～してもよろしいですか〔許可〕）「クッダイ」、Could you ...?（～していただけますか〔依頼〕）「クッジュー」、Why not ...?（～したらどうですか〔提案〕）「(ホ)ワィノッ(ト)」といった音声に慣れておきましょう。

- **Part 3** で Peter Franklin という名前が出てきますが、これは設問とは関係がありません。設問を見ていなければ、必要のない情報にまで注意を払わなければなりません。あらかじめ何を聞き取ればいいのか理解しておくと正答率はぐっと上がります。会話問題攻略のコツは、会話が始まる前に設問を見ておくことです。

Unit 9 The Weather

Warm-up

Check 1 Match the words to the definitions. Write the letters on the lines.

1. shower   _____   a. slightly cold
2. thunder   _____   b. light rain
3. freeze   _____   c. loud noise you hear during a storm
4. chilly   _____   d. thick cloud that makes it difficult to see
5. fog   _____   e. to turn into ice or become very cold

Check 2 Choose the correct word or phrase from the box to complete each sentence.

| clear up | high-pressure | humid | unpredictable | weather forecast |

1. The weather changes quickly and is (   ) at this time of year.
2. I hope the weather will (   ) tomorrow, because we want to go hiking.
3. I listened to the (   ) this morning. It will be sunny on Sunday.
4. When a (   ) system comes into your region, it brings fine weather.
5. When it is (   ) outside, you feel uncomfortable because the air is wet and hot.

Test Questions

Part 1 Photographs   34

1.   Ⓐ Ⓑ Ⓒ Ⓓ

2.   Ⓐ Ⓑ Ⓒ Ⓓ

Part 2 Question-Response 　　🔵 35

3. Mark your answer.　　　　　　　　　Ⓐ　Ⓑ　Ⓒ
4. Mark your answer.　　　　　　　　　Ⓐ　Ⓑ　Ⓒ

Part 3 Short Conversations 　　🔵 36

5. When can we expect rain?
    (A) Before lunch　　　　　　(B) Early in the morning
    (C) In the afternoon　　　　 (D) Not today

6. What is the forecaster not sure of?
    (A) If it will be fine
    (B) If there will be showers
    (C) If there will be thunder and lightning
    (D) If it will be rainy

7. What does the man hope to do?
    (A) Go roller-skating　　　　(B) Go for a hike
    (C) The forecaster is right.　(D) Stay at home

Part 4 Short Talks 　　🔵 37

8. What activity did the forecaster suggest doing on Sunday?
    (A) Clean the house　　　　(B) Wash and hang out the laundry
    (C) Go hiking　　　　　　　(D) Wash the car

9. Which area is NOT going to have good weather on Sunday?
    (A) All of King county　　　(B) The mountains in the south
    (C) The areas along the coast (D) The hills in the north

10. What warning did the forecaster give listeners?
    (A) The wind will be quite strong.　(B) Don't work too hard.
    (C) Don't get a sunburn.　　　　　(D) Avoid the hills.

Follow-up

写真問題攻略のコツ (2)

- **Part 1** の relaxing in the shade (木陰でくつろいでいる)は「リラクスィンインザシェイド」と聞こえます。写真問題では動作動詞は進行形で表されることがよくあります。
- relaxing in ... のように進行形に使われる動詞の -ing 形の [g] は消えやすい音で、後ろに母音で始まる単語が来ると音がつながります。
- 写真問題攻略のコツは、人物が写っている場合には人物の動作をよく見て動詞をしっかり聞き取ることです。

25

Unit 10 Education

Warm-up

Check 1 Match the words to the definitions. Write the letters on the lines.

1. major   _____   a. private instructor
2. degree   _____   b. unit of study
3. tuition _____   c. university student's special field of study
4. credit   _____   d. certificate or title showing college graduation
5. tutor   _____   e. money paid for classes or lessons

Check 2 Choose the correct word or phrase from the box to complete each sentence.

| graduates | liberal arts | higher education | psychology | study abroad |

1. Some students (_____) to expand their language and cultural understanding.
2. A (_____) education makes for well-rounded people.
3. Are you planning to go on to (_____) after high school?
4. Hundreds of business school (_____) are working in this company.
5. Mike wanted to learn more about human behavior, so he majored in (_____) at university.

Test Questions

Part 1 Photographs   38

1.   2.

   Ⓐ Ⓑ Ⓒ Ⓓ   Ⓐ Ⓑ Ⓒ Ⓓ

26

Part 2 Question-Response   39

3. Mark your answer.   Ⓐ Ⓑ Ⓒ
4. Mark your answer.   Ⓐ Ⓑ Ⓒ

Part 3 Short Conversations   40

5. When did the man make up his mind about what he wanted to do?
   (A) A teacher
   (B) When he started university
   (C) Only recently
   (D) A long time ago

6. How did the woman choose her major?
   (A) Her teacher advised her.
   (B) Her mother and father advised her.
   (C) She needs a job.
   (D) She always dreamed about it.

7. How is the woman getting on in her studies?
   (A) Business is fascinating.
   (B) English is hard for her.
   (C) English is OK but not business.
   (D) She's changing her major.

Part 4 Short Talks   41

8. What was the teacher's problem?
   (A) Two students were behaving badly.
   (B) A boy and girl were texting each other.
   (C) Some of the students were sleeping.
   (D) Most of his students dislike geography.

9. When does the teacher say this kind of problem started?
   (A) Only recently
   (B) It's been around for years.
   (C) The teacher did it when she was young.
   (D) It's society's fault.

10. If the speaker punishes them, how does she think they will react?
    (A) They will apologize.
    (B) They will complain.
    (C) They will behave better.
    (D) They will change teachers.

Follow-up

会話問題攻略のコツ (2)

- Part 3 の but I'm bored ...（しかし、〜に退屈している）は「バタイムボァ(ド)」と聞こえます。会話問題攻略のコツは、男性と女性の会話なので、どのセリフがどちらの主張なのかを性別を区別して聞くことです。設問 5 は男性、設問 6 と 7 は女性の発話に注意して聞きましょう。
- 会話問題では I と you が頻繁に使われるので、2 人の関係をイメージしながら聞くことが大切です。
- I と you は前の単語の語尾の音と同化して、1 つの音のように発音されます。また音声変化が生じる場合もあります。But I ... 「バダイ」、When I ... 「ウェナイ」、Can't you ... 「キャンチュー」Would you ... 「ウッジュー」など、よく出てくる音声に慣れておきましょう。

Unit 11 Fitness

Warm-up

Check 1 What verb do you use for these words? Put the words in the appropriate boxes.

> aerobics   basketball   a bicycle   a boat   golf
> a horse   jogging   push-ups   sit-ups   a skateboard
> skating   skiing   soccer   swimming   tennis   yoga

do	play	ride	go

Check 2 Match the questions or comments (1-5) with the responses (a-e). Write the letters on the lines.

1. How often do you go to the gym? _____   a. I exercise a lot.
2. How much time do I need to do this exercise? _____   b. So so, I guess.
3. I'm at the ER. I think I broke my leg. _____   c. Twenty more minutes.
4. Is your diet healthy? _____   d. Three times a week.
5. What do you do to stay healthy? _____   e. Oh, no! Are you badly hurt?

Test Questions

Part 1 Photographs   42

1. Ⓐ Ⓑ Ⓒ Ⓓ

2. Ⓐ Ⓑ Ⓒ Ⓓ

28

Part 2 Question-Response　　43

3. Mark your answer.　　Ⓐ Ⓑ Ⓒ
4. Mark your answer.　　Ⓐ Ⓑ Ⓒ

Part 3. Short Conversations　　44

5. How much exercise is the woman doing?
    (A) An hour each day
    (B) Every other day
    (C) Twice a week
    (D) Not nearly enough

6. What has the man noticed about the woman?
    (A) She moves around more quickly.
    (B) She's an excellent dancer.
    (C) She has put a little weight.
    (D) She looks healthier and fitter.

7. What problem does the woman have?
    (A) Her clothes are too big.
    (B) She feels hungry all the time.
    (C) Her clothes are too small.
    (D) She wants to sleep all day.

Part 4 Short Talks　　45

8. Which of these is NOT mentioned as a benefit for students doing sports?
    (A) Improved strength
    (B) Better fitness
    (C) They learn to cooperate.
    (D) Increased popularity

9. How does doing sports affect students' grades?
    (A) They become too competitive.
    (B) They do better.
    (C) They are often too tired to study.
    (D) So far, no effect has been seen.

10. What does the school make sure of?
    (A) That every student is an excellent athlete
    (B) That no student is forced to take part in sports
    (C) That every student takes part in at least one team sport
    (D) That sports doesn't affect students' academic work

Follow-up

応答問題攻略のコツ (1)

- Part 2 の What's wrong?（どうしたのですか）は「ワッツロン(グ)」と聞こえます。会話でよく使用される表現です。このような慣用的な表現を身につけることが大切です。
- 応答問題攻略のコツは、まずは会話の自然なやり取りに慣れることです。What's wrong? と相手を心配する言葉に対して、ふつうは I have a headache.（頭痛がします）と悪い事柄で答えるのが自然な応答です。逆に I'm better today.（今日は元気です）のような、気遣う相手の言葉を無視した応答はしません。

Unit 12   Mini Test 2

Part 1   Photographs   46

1.   Ⓐ Ⓑ Ⓒ Ⓓ

2.   Ⓐ Ⓑ Ⓒ Ⓓ

3.   Ⓐ Ⓑ Ⓒ Ⓓ

4.   Ⓐ Ⓑ Ⓒ Ⓓ

Part 2   Question-Response   47

5. Mark your answer.   Ⓐ Ⓑ Ⓒ

6. Mark your answer.   Ⓐ Ⓑ Ⓒ

7. Mark your answer.   Ⓐ Ⓑ Ⓒ

8. Mark your answer.   Ⓐ Ⓑ Ⓒ

9. Mark your answer.   Ⓐ Ⓑ Ⓒ

Part 3 Short Conversations 48

10. When did the man book his room?
    (A) He paid in advance.
    (B) He is checking in right now.
    (C) Probably a couple of hours ago
    (D) Two nights ago

11. How did the man book his room?
    (A) He came here in person.
    (B) He sent a fax.
    (C) Over the Internet
    (D) He called.

12. When is the man checking out?
    (A) Monday
    (B) Tuesday
    (C) Wednesday
    (D) Thursday

Part 4 Short Talks 49

13. Why don't you feel cold in the morning with just a T-shirt on?
    (A) Climbing makes you hot.
    (B) It's warm at the bottom of the mountain.
    (C) The mountains are warm all summer long.
    (D) It's always sunny on top of the mountain.

14. What makes the temperature drop?
    (A) The higher altitude
    (B) The sudden strong wind
    (C) The mountains blocking the sun
    (D) The poor air quality

15. What does the wind-chill factor do?
    (A) Shuts out the wind
    (B) Makes it seem warmer
    (C) Makes warm clothes necessary
    (D) Makes rainwear unnecessary

Unit 13 Business Trips

Warm-up

Check 1 Match the words to the definitions. Write the letters on the lines.

1. economy   _____   a. official document that shows one's nationality
2. insurance   _____   b. less expensive seating area in an airplane
3. currency   _____   c. steel box with a lock, usually with a combination
4. safe   _____   d. money used in a certain country
5. passport   _____   e. financial protection for unforeseen trouble

Check 2 Choose the correct word from the box to complete each sentence.

| flight | rent | show | seated | shuttle |

1. Please remain (   ) until the aircraft comes to a complete stop.
2. I will (   ) a car at the airport when I arrive in San Francisco.
3. I have decided to take an early (   ) back to Los Angeles this afternoon.
4. The bellboy will take your luggage and (   ) you to your room.
5. At the airport, we can catch a (   ) bus that will take us to the hotel.

Test Questions

Part 1 Photographs   50

1. Ⓐ Ⓑ Ⓒ Ⓓ

2. Ⓐ Ⓑ Ⓒ Ⓓ

Part 2 Question-Response　　　51

3. Mark your answer.　　　Ⓐ　Ⓑ　Ⓒ
4. Mark your answer.　　　Ⓐ　Ⓑ　Ⓒ

Part 3 Short Conversations　　　52

5. Where does this conversation take place?
   - (A) At a train station
   - (B) At an airport arrival lobby
   - (C) At an airport departure area
   - (D) At a hotel

6. What does the woman want to know?
   - (A) If she should go to the office now
   - (B) Where the office is
   - (C) How long it takes to get to the hotel
   - (D) What time the meeting starts

7. What will the man do tomorrow morning?
   - (A) Start the meeting
   - (B) Take the woman to her hotel
   - (C) Take the woman to the office
   - (D) Give the woman a wake-up call at 7:00

Part 4 Short Talks　　　53

8. What kind of accommodation should business travelers use?
   - (A) Only those hotels approved by the company
   - (B) Hotels near the office
   - (C) Luxury hotels
   - (D) Inexpensive hotels

9. What does the announcement generally recommend?
   - (A) Being economical
   - (B) Eating in fast-food restaurant
   - (C) Taking taxis everywhere
   - (D) Staying near the office

10. What must business travelers do to get reimbursed for their expenses?
    - (A) Meet with the accounting department
    - (B) Hand in their claim quickly
    - (C) Save their receipts and fill out the proper forms
    - (D) Simply hand in their receipts

Follow-up

ショートトーク問題攻略のコツ (1)

- リスニングの前に、何についてのトークであるのかを、前もって知っておくことがショートトーク問題攻略のコツです。そのため、あらかじめ設問と選択肢に目を通しておきましょう。
- Part 4 の設問と選択肢に business travelers, hotels, taxis といった語句があります。つまりナレーションは出張に関するものだと推測できます。
- Part 4 の選択肢の reimburse（返金する）や receipt（レシート）のような単語から旅行費用の請求の話だとわかります。ノーヒントでいきなり聞くよりもずっと容易に内容を聞き取ることができます。

Unit 14　Production and Sales

Warm-up

Check 1　To what category do these things belong? Put the words in the appropriate boxes.

> announcement　　assembly line　　bidding　　campaign
> charge　　commercial　　factory　　in stock
> poster　　purchase discount　　raw materials　　tag

Advertising	Price	Production

Check 2　Match the questions or comments (1-5) with the responses (a-e). Write the letters on the lines.

1. What is this made of?　　_____
2. Did sales increase at all?　　_____
3. What can we do to boost sales?　　_____
4. Why did production fall again?　　_____
5. We should stop production immediately.　　_____

a. Yes, but only slightly, by 0.5%.
b. We had a problem with quality control.
c. Iron and copper, mainly.
d. I don't agree with you.
e. How about offering big discounts?

Test Questions

Part 1　Photographs　　　54

1.　　　　　　　　　　　　　2.

Ⓐ　Ⓑ　Ⓒ　Ⓓ　　　　　　　Ⓐ　Ⓑ　Ⓒ　Ⓓ

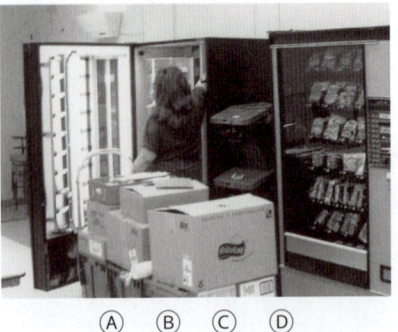

34

Part 2   Question-Response　　　　　　　　　🎧 55

3. Mark your answer.　　　　　　　　　　　Ⓐ Ⓑ Ⓒ
4. Mark your answer.　　　　　　　　　　　Ⓐ Ⓑ Ⓒ

Part 3   Short Conversations　　　　　　　　🎧 56

5. What caused the increase in sales?
   - (A) A larger sales staff
   - (B) Better products
   - (C) The boss's orders
   - (D) Effective advertising

6. What does the woman say is going to be promoted next?
   - (A) Ski equipment
   - (B) Outdoor goods
   - (C) Fall and winter items
   - (D) Camping goods

7. What is the man's reaction?
   - (A) He wants to help.
   - (B) He is disappointed.
   - (C) He is encouraging his staff.
   - (D) He is surprised.

Part 4   Short Talks　　　　　　　　　　　🎧 57

8. What does the speaker want the new sales pitches to be like?
   - (A) Long and complicated
   - (B) Annoying
   - (C) Loud and colorful
   - (D) Short and to the point

9. What will the sales campaign aim for?
   - (A) High volume, low prices
   - (B) Low volume, high prices
   - (C) Long term sales
   - (D) High quality, high prices

10. Which of these slogans would fit the campaign?
    - (A) Buy now, pay later!
    - (B) Well made and always in fashion
    - (C) 50% discount on all swimwear
    - (D) Back to school sale!

Follow-up

応答問題攻略のコツ (2)

- **Part 2** に Certainly.（承知しました）「サートンリィ」と言う音声が聞こえます。目上の人やお客様に Could you bring me a glass of water?（水を1杯持ってきてくれますか）と依頼されたとき、会話では Sure.（もちろんです）や Certainly.（承知しました）のような応答がよくあります。

- Yes/No で答える疑問文でも、必ずしも Yes/No が使われるとは限らないのです。応答問題攻略のコツは会話の自然な流れと共に、頻繁に出題される応答のフレーズを覚えることが必要です。

Unit 15 — Job Hunting and Recruitment

Warm-up

Check 1 Match the words to the definitions. Write the letters on the lines.

1. résumé   _____   a. to find new people to work
2. qualifications _____   b. position to be filled
3. trainee   _____   c. paper showing one's education and experience
4. vacancy   _____   d. education, skills, experience, etc. needed for a job
5. recruit   _____   e. person learning a job

Check 2 Match the questions (1-5) with the responses (a-e). Write the letters on the lines.

1. How about we set up a pasta franchise?   _____   a. No, it's casual dress.
2. Do we have to wear a uniform at work?   _____   b. I'm with General Motors.
3. Who do you work for?   _____   c. Yes, they don't have enough experience.
4. Would you be able to work a late shift? _____   d. No, I'm not interested in restaurants.
5. Do you have a problem with our applicants? _____ e. Sorry, but I already have plans.

Test Questions

Part 1 Photographs   58

1.   Ⓐ Ⓑ Ⓒ Ⓓ

2.   Ⓐ Ⓑ Ⓒ Ⓓ

Part 2 Question-Response 🔵 59

3. Mark your answer. Ⓐ Ⓑ Ⓒ
4. Mark your answer. Ⓐ Ⓑ Ⓒ

Part 3 Short Conversations 🔵 60

5. How long did the woman work at the previous company?
   (A) About a decade (B) Around 12 years
   (C) More than 20 years (D) Nearly 30 years

6. What happened to the woman's job?
   (A) A younger person took it. (B) She was fired.
   (C) She quit on her own. (D) The company went bankrupt.

7. What kind of work did the woman do after she lost her job?
   (A) All kinds (B) Only office work
   (C) Sales (D) She was unemployed.

Part 4 Short Talks 🔵 61

8. What kind of work will the person be expected to do?
   (A) Running errands (B) Telephone sales
   (C) Greeting guests (D) Writing, computing, talking on the phone

9. What did the speaker say about arriving late?
   (A) Don't do it too often. (B) It's not permitted.
   (C) It's only allowed in the mornings. (D) It will cost the worker his or her job.

10. When will the employee be asked to work overtime?
    (A) When he or she wants to earn extra money
    (B) When the company needs someone to be confident on the phone
    (C) When a delivery needs to be made in a hurry
    (D) On weekends

Follow-up

ショートトーク問題の攻略 (2)

- **Part 4** に must be punctual（時間厳守しなければならない）「マス(ト)ビィパンクチャゥ」と聞こえる語句があります。これは言いかえれば Arriving late is not permitted.（遅れて来ることは許されない）のことで、ナレーションの punctual と同じ意味です。
- ナレーションで使われている表現が、印刷されている選択肢の中では言い換えた表現をしていることがよくあります。ショートトーク問題攻略のコツは、類義語や同じ意味の表現に慣れておくことです。
- **Part 4** の work late（遅くまで働く）「ワークレイ(ト)」が、設問で work overtime（残業する）と表現されています。このような語句の言い換えに気をつけましょう。

Unit 16　Accounting

Warm-up

Check 1　Match the words to the definitions. Write the letters on the lines.

1. capital　　　　_____　　a. having to do with money
2. accountant　　_____　　b. act of selling and buying an item
3. financial　　　_____　　c. income or money earned
4. transaction　　_____　　d. money invested in a business
5. revenue　　　 _____　　e. expert at money, taxes, etc.

Check 2　Choose the correct word from the box to complete each sentence.

> balance　　debits　　deposited　　financial　　recording

1. Managers depend on accountants to provide them with information about the company's (　　　　) condition.

2. A company's balance sheet is a record of its (　　　　) and credits.

3. Bookkeeping records must be examined to ensure that they (　　　　) correctly.

4. Accountants are responsible for (　　　　) a company's financial activity.

5. My salary is (　　　　) into my bank account at the end of each month.

Test Questions

Part 1　Photographs　　　　　　　　　　　　　　　　62

1.　　Ⓐ　Ⓑ　Ⓒ　Ⓓ

2.　　Ⓐ　Ⓑ　Ⓒ　Ⓓ

38

Part 2 Question-Response   63

3. Mark your answer. Ⓐ Ⓑ Ⓒ
4. Mark your answer. Ⓐ Ⓑ Ⓒ

Part 3 Short Conversations   64

5. What is the problem with Mr. Pearson?
   (A) He has been complaining about his job.
   (B) He forgets things.
   (C) He's a qualified accountant.
   (D) He makes quite a few errors.

6. Who will be finding Mr. Pearson a new position in the company?
   (A) Peter
   (B) The Personnel Affairs section
   (C) The General Affairs section
   (D) The Accounting Department

7. What do we know about Peter?
   (A) He has a lot of experience.
   (B) He just started working last month.
   (C) He seems to be good at his job.
   (D) He works in the accounting office.

Part 4 Short Talks   65

8. What has the interviewer heard about Peter?
   (A) He gets on well with his colleagues.
   (B) He hasn't settled in yet.
   (C) He is a good worker.
   (D) He loves accounting.

9. What kind of person is accounts looking for?
   (A) A person who is good with numbers
   (B) Someone to teach accounting
   (C) A person with a college accounting degree
   (D) A young person

10. What must Peter agree to do if he wants the job?
    (A) Work at night
    (B) Take his time making his decision
    (C) Promise to work hard
    (D) Study accounting after work

Follow-up

応答問題の攻略 (3)

- Part 2 に When is the deadline...?（締め切りはいつですか）「ウェンイ(ズ)ザデッ(ド)ライン」があります。応答問題では最初の文が疑問文であることが多く、特に疑問詞（What, When, Where, Who, Which, Why, How）がよく使われますので、最初を聞き逃さないように集中することが応答問題攻略のコツです。

- Where と聞こえたら「場所」、When と聞こえたら「時間」を答えるのが自然な会話の流れです。しかし I don't know.（知りません）と答えてもやはり自然な流れですので注意してください。

Unit 17 Personnel

Warm-up

Check 1   Match the words to the definitions. Write the letters on the lines.

1. promotion   _____   a. to move to a new place of employment
2. relocate   _____   b. move to a higher or more important position
3. lay off   _____   c. to examine and judge carefully
4. colleague   _____   d. to dismiss from employment
5. evaluate   _____   e. coworker

Check 2   Choose the correct word from the box to complete each sentence.

| fair | headhunters | notice | retirement | transfer |

1. Recruiters look for new employees and they are also called (   ).

2. When you leave a job, you should give at least two weeks' (   ).

3. We would like to (   ) you to our New York branch.

4. The committee decided that the manager's treatment of the clerk was (   ) and completely justified.

5. Older staff members are planning what they will do after (   ).

Test Questions

Part 1   Photographs   66

1.   2.

  Ⓐ Ⓑ Ⓒ Ⓓ   Ⓐ Ⓑ Ⓒ Ⓓ

40

Part 2   Question-Response   🔵 67

3. Mark your answer.   Ⓐ Ⓑ Ⓒ
4. Mark your answer.   Ⓐ Ⓑ Ⓒ

Part 3   Short Conversations   🔵 68

5. How does the woman feel about where she works?
   (A) It is too crowded.
   (B) She is not happy.
   (C) She is too busy.
   (D) She has to stand up too long each day.

6. What did the man assume?
   (A) That the woman was happy in her job
   (B) That the woman liked Brenda and Linda
   (C) That the woman had already left
   (D) That the woman was a good worker

7. How does the man react to the woman's problem?
   (A) He says it must be Brenda's fault.
   (B) He thinks the woman is being foolish.
   (C) He tells the woman what to do.
   (D) He agrees that what Brenda and Linda are doing is wrong.

Part 4   Short Talks   🔵 69

8. What is the cause of the office problem?
   (A) The staff aren't doing their jobs.
   (B) Some staff are antisocial.
   (C) The office is too small.
   (D) The cliques are doing most of the work.

9. What does the speaker demand that workers try to do?
   (A) Be more friendly
   (B) Obey the rules
   (C) Be more punctual
   (D) Work harder

10. What is the speaker threatening to do?
    (A) To advise workers
    (B) To form new cliques
    (C) To transfer or fire employees
    (D) To reduce workers' salaries

Follow-up

英語耳

- **Part 3** の I can't stand（〜を我慢できない）は、「アイキャン・スタン(ド)」と聞こえます。この can't のように否定の短縮形の [t] は消えることがよくあります。[t] 音が消失してあたかも I can のように聞こえますが、can't は次の単語の語頭の前に一瞬の間が生じます。音の間や強弱など音全体で理解するようにしましょう。
- 音声変化を知識として知っているだけでなく、英語を毎日聞き流すことで英語耳を作ることができます。スポーツで体を鍛えるように、耳を鍛えるリスニングトレーニングをしましょう。

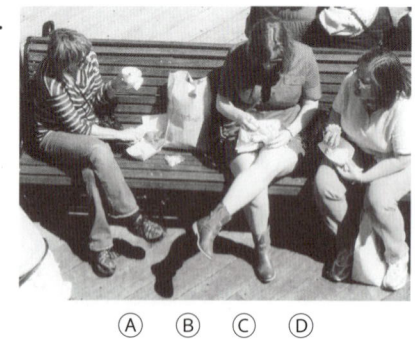

Unit 18　Mini Test 3

Part 1　Photographs　　　　　　　　　　　　　　　　　　　　　70

1.　Ⓐ Ⓑ Ⓒ Ⓓ

2.　Ⓐ Ⓑ Ⓒ Ⓓ

3.　Ⓐ Ⓑ Ⓒ Ⓓ

4.　Ⓐ Ⓑ Ⓒ Ⓓ

Part 2　Question-Response　　　　　　　　　　　　　　　　　71

5. Mark your answer.　　　　　　　　　　　　Ⓐ Ⓑ Ⓒ
6. Mark your answer.　　　　　　　　　　　　Ⓐ Ⓑ Ⓒ
7. Mark your answer.　　　　　　　　　　　　Ⓐ Ⓑ Ⓒ
8. Mark your answer.　　　　　　　　　　　　Ⓐ Ⓑ Ⓒ
9. Mark your answer.　　　　　　　　　　　　Ⓐ Ⓑ Ⓒ

Part 3 Short Conversations　　　　　　　　　　　　　　　　　　72

10. What caused Pamela to hand in her notice?
    (A) A family illness
    (B) A financial problem
    (C) A new job
    (D) A schedule conflict

11. How does the man feel about Pamela?
    (A) It can't be helped.
    (B) She is not really necessary to the company.
    (C) She is unreliable.
    (D) Nobody is a better worker than she.

12. How long will the temp work at the company?
    (A) Until a permanent worker can be found
    (B) She will stay permanently.
    (C) Until Pamela's mother gets better
    (D) Only if she works hard

Part 4 Short Talks　　　　　　　　　　　　　　　　　　　　73

13. What is the purpose of Brian's visit to CleanAll?
    (A) To try to get a more favorable price
    (B) To have a job interview
    (C) To sell brush sets
    (D) To introduce a new product

14. Where is Brian heading on Wednesday?
    (A) To Houston
    (B) To CleanAll
    (C) To his company's Atlanta office
    (D) To another company in Atlanta

15. When will Brian book his hotel and flights?
    (A) As soon as he arrives in Houston
    (B) Before he takes the subway
    (C) On Wednesday morning
    (D) The office has already taken care of that.

Unit 19 Customer Service

Warm-up

Check 1 Match the words to the definitions. Write the letters on the lines.

1. complain   ____   a. fault in something such as a product
2. inconvenience ____   b. written promise to replace a product if it is faulty
3. defect   ____   c. to find an acceptable solution to a problem
4. resolve   ____   d. something that is troublesome
5. warranty   ____   e. to say something is wrong

Check 2 Match the questions or comments (1-5) with the responses (a-e). Write the letters on the lines.

1. Why didn't the order arrive?   ____   a. What seems to be the problem?
2. I have a serious complaint.   ____   b. They can exchange them.
3. The price is wrong.   ____   c. You should call them about the problem.
4. What's the best thing to do now?   ____   d. They sent it to the wrong address.
5. The items we received were damaged.   ____   e. I'll check with the accounts section.

Test Questions

Part 1 Photographs   74

1. Ⓐ Ⓑ Ⓒ Ⓓ

2. Ⓐ Ⓑ Ⓒ Ⓓ

44

Part 2 Question-Response　　　　　　　　　　　　　　　　　75

3. Mark your answer.　　　　　　　　　　　　　　Ⓐ　Ⓑ　Ⓒ
4. Mark your answer.　　　　　　　　　　　　　　Ⓐ　Ⓑ　Ⓒ

Part 3 Short Conversations　　　　　　　　　　　　　　　76

5. What are people complaining about?
    (A) The drivers are too rude.　　(B) The goods are damaged.
    (C) The goods arrive late.　　　(D) The price is too high.

6. What is the cause of the problem?
    (A) One of the trucks broke down.　　(B) One driver is often late for work.
    (C) Traffic is always heavy.　　　　　(D) There is a shortage of goods.

7. What will happen to the driver?
    (A) He will have to apologize to the customers.
    (B) He will have to pay a fine.
    (C) He will be replaced.
    (D) He will have to work harder.

Part 4 Short Talks　　　　　　　　　　　　　　　　　　　77

8. What word is used to describe good customer service?
    (A) Fake　　　　　　　　　　(B) Ideal
    (C) Vital　　　　　　　　　　(D) Worse

9. Why might a business not be successful, according to the speaker?
    (A) If it doesn't cut prices　　　　　　(B) If customers don't come back
    (C) If it doesn't offer sales promotions　(D) If it offers poor products

10. What does the speaker say is the most important in customer service?
    (A) Excellent management　　　(B) Advertising
    (C) New customers　　　　　　(D) Well-trained staff

Follow-up

短縮形

- **Part 2** に「ゼアズ」「アイル」「アイム」と聞こえる短縮形があります。それぞれ There's, I'll, I'm のことです。話し言葉の音声的特徴の1つである短縮形は意味を理解する上で重要なので、文脈からも判断して正確に聞き取るようにしましょう。

- 短縮形の例
    (1) **主語 + be 動詞・助動詞**
        he's → he is, he has　　it's → it is, it has　　I'd → I had, I would
    (2) **疑問詞・there + be 動詞・助動詞**
        what's → what is, what has　who's → who is, who has　there's → there is, there has
    (3) **be 動詞・助動詞 + not**
        aren't → are not　　doesn't → does not　　won't → will not

---

45

Unit 20   Order and Shipping

Warm-up

Check 1   Match the words to the definitions. Write the letters on the lines.

1. cargo   _____   a. to make a statement of taxable goods
2. ship   _____   b. goods that are being transported
3. declare   _____   c. huge box to hold goods for transport
4. customs   _____   d. to send by land, sea or air
5. container   _____   e. government tax on imported goods

Check 2   Choose the correct word from the box to complete each sentence.

| buyer | perishable | destination | export | trustworthy |

1. The transportation company provides the best service, and it must be (   ).

2. The (   ) goods will be shipped in a temperature-controlled container tomorrow.

3. An invoice is a document issued by a seller to a (   ) that states the product being shipped and its price and quantity.

4. When the goods have arrived at the (   ), a true weight quantity is determined.

5. Countries import goods from abroad and (   ) others to the rest of the world.

Test Questions

Part 1 Photographs   78

1.

     Ⓐ Ⓑ Ⓒ Ⓓ

2.

     Ⓐ Ⓑ Ⓒ Ⓓ

46

Part 2 Question-Response 79

3. Mark your answer. Ⓐ Ⓑ Ⓒ
4. Mark your answer. Ⓐ Ⓑ Ⓒ

Part 3 Short Conversations 80

5. How many medium-sized coffee makers would most likely fit in a standard shipping box?
   (A) Four (B) Fewer than four
   (C) More than four (D) Four or five

6. How many boxes will they have to send?
   (A) 30 (B) 40 (C) 50 (D) 200

7. How will the company fill the order?
   (A) By waiting one week (B) By increasing production
   (C) By making two shipments (D) By using goods in their two warehouses

Part 4 Short Talks 81

8. What does efficiency refer to?
   (A) Without any problems (B) Being trustworthy
   (C) Attracting customers (D) Without wasting time

9. What does the speaker say should never happen?
   (A) Small orders (B) Large orders
   (C) The tiniest scratch on a product (D) Early arrivals

10. How does the speaker say the company can achieve its quality control goals?
    (A) By everyone pulling together (B) By delivering goods by hand
    (C) By working overtime (D) Through proper training

Follow-up

綴りと発音

- **Part 2** の improve our packing（包装を改善する）は「インプルーヴアワパキン」と聞こえます。packing は「パキング」ではなく「パキン」と発音します。ローマ字読みで綴り通りに発音するのではなく、綴りと発音が異なるときがあるので注意しましょう。
- 綴りから判断してよく間違う発音：

	発音記号	誤	正
work（働く）	wə́:rk	ウォーク	ワーク
award（賞）	əwɔ́:rd	アワード	アウォード
package（包み）	pǽkidʒ	パッケージ	パキッヂ
baggage（手荷物）	bǽgidʒ	バッゲージ	バギッヂ
damage（損害）	dǽmidʒ	ダメージ	ダミッヂ

Unit 21 Negotiations

Warm-up

Check 1 Match the words to the definitions. Write the letters on the lines.

1. impulse _____
2. haggle _____
3. cooperate _____
4. consensus _____
5. resolve _____

a. to try to get a cheaper price
b. to come to an agreement or find a solution
c. quick decision made without much thought
d. to work together
e. agreement by everyone

Check 2 Match the questions or comments (1-5) with the responses (a-e). Write the letters on the lines.

1. What sort of quantities are you looking for? _____
2. What reduction could we receive? _____
3. I appreciate everything you have done. _____
4. What do you think of our proposal? _____
5. What about the negotiations with Mr. Parker? _____

a. It's a good idea, but it might be expensive.
b. We haven't come to an agreement yet.
c. We could offer you a five percent discount.
d. Thanks, it's been my pleasure.
e. We are considering 8,000 units.

Test Questions

Part 1 Photographs   82

1.   Ⓐ Ⓑ Ⓒ Ⓓ

2.   Ⓐ Ⓑ Ⓒ Ⓓ

Part 2   Question-Response   🔵 83

3. Mark your answer.   Ⓐ Ⓑ Ⓒ
4. Mark your answer.   Ⓐ Ⓑ Ⓒ

Part 3   Short Conversations   🔵 84

5. What seems to be the problem with the transport company?
    (A) It makes late deliveries and is careless with the goods.
    (B) It often delivers to the wrong address.
    (C) Its trucks often break down.
    (D) The delivery personnel are impolite and inefficient.

6. Under a new contract, what would happen if goods arrived damaged?
    (A) The customer would get a refund.
    (B) The company would cancel the contract.
    (C) This driver would be fired.
    (D) The company would impose a sanction.

7. How much would the company refuse to pay if some goods were damaged in shipment?
    (A) It would delay payment.   (B) Twenty-five percent of the bill
    (C) Seventy-five percent of the bill (D) The full amount of the bill

Part 4   Short Talks   🔵 85

8. What did the present transport company refuse to do?
    (A) Attend the meeting   (B) Give a refund
    (C) Agree to the company's proposals (D) Replace damaged goods

9. What did the speaker do after negotiating with the present transport company?
    (A) He found a new company.   (B) He hired temporary employees.
    (C) He moved to a different city.   (D) He negotiated with them again.

10. What is the good news for the speaker?
    (A) He disliked the old company.
    (B) They can't find a replacement.
    (C) The old company finally agreed.
    (D) The new company seems to be much more reliable.

Follow-up

音の同化

- **Part 2** の has to be rewritten（書き直さなければなりません）は「ハストゥビィリリトン」と聞こえます。has to は「ハストゥ」、have to は「ハフトゥ」、had to は「ハットゥ」と、音が連結するとき、隣接音に影響されて前の音が違った音〔無声音〕に変化します。このような音声変化を音の同化と言います。
- write は過去形・過去分詞形が不規則変化して write-wrote-written となりますが、written は「リトン」と発音します。

Unit 22 Presentations

Warm-up

Check 1 Match the words to the definitions. Write the letters on the lines.

1. visual aids _____
2. handout _____
3. chart _____
4. rehearse _____
5. topic _____

a. information in the form of a table or graph
b. to practice for a presentation
c. subject of a speech
d. written information given to people in an audience
e. various materials or tools used in teaching

Check 2 Match the questions (1-5) with the responses (a-e). Write the letters on the lines.

1. Who prepared that data? _____
2. Have you made your presentation yet? _____
3. Can we ask questions in the middle of the talk? _____
4. How long did it take you to finish your speech? _____
5. Where is this month's conference being held? _____

a. I heard it is in Boston.
b. Just about one hour.
c. Yes, and everything went very well.
d. Yes, please feel free to do so.
e. John and I worked on it together.

Test Questions

Part 1 Photographs 86

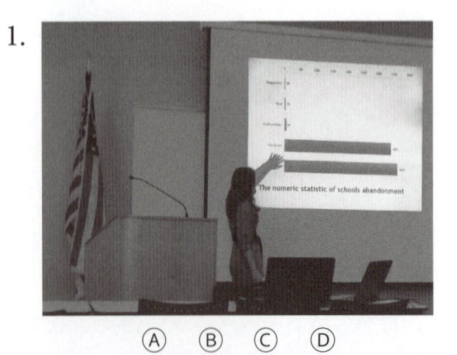

1.

Ⓐ Ⓑ Ⓒ Ⓓ

2.

Ⓐ Ⓑ Ⓒ Ⓓ

50

Part 2　Question-Response　　　　　　　　　　　　　🔊 87

3. Mark your answer.　　　　　　　　　　Ⓐ　Ⓑ　Ⓒ
4. Mark your answer.　　　　　　　　　　Ⓐ　Ⓑ　Ⓒ

Part 3　Short Conversations　　　　　　　　　　　🔊 88

5. What is the man's first question about?
   (A) Competitors' brushes
   (B) What type of brush the woman sells
   (C) Why the woman's brushes are worth buying
   (D) Who makes the brushes

6. What advantage of the brush does the woman mention first?
   (A) Its name　　　　　　　　(B) Its comfort
   (C) Its low price　　　　　　(D) Its range of colors

7. Why does the woman say the brushes function so well?
   (A) They are inexpensive.　　　　(B) They are small and easy to use.
   (C) They are very strong.　　　　(D) They are adjustable.

Part 4　Short Talks　　　　　　　　　　　　　　　🔊 89

8. What does the speaker NOT mention about the brush set?
   (A) The color　　(B) The function　　(C) The weight　　(D) The shape

9. What does the speaker mean by "innovative"?
   (A) Regular　　(B) Ordinary　　(C) Inexpensive　　(D) Unique

10. Which of these is NOT true?
    (A) The brushes come in six different colors.
    (B) The brushes can clean around corners and chair legs.
    (C) Some of the brushes are curved.
    (D) If you order a set today, you can get another set of brushes for the garden absolutely free.

Follow-up

数字の読み方

- **Part 4** の half a dozen は「ハーファダズン」と聞こえます。TOEIC® では正確に時間や数字を聞き取る必要があります。時刻表現の基本は時と分の数字を並べて at 3:20「アッスリートウェンティ」と発音します。ちなみにアメリカ英語では twenty の [nt] は、2つ音が影響し合って同化し、1つの [n] 音になり「トウェニィ」と聞こえることがあります。
- 年号：1990 は nineteen ninety、2003 は two thousand (and) three、2014 は twenty fourteen
- 小数点：[.] は point「ポイント」と読み、0.3 は zero point three
- 値段：$9.99 は nine dollars (and) ninety-nine (cents) または nine ninety-nine
- 数を表す表現：quarter（25セント、15分）「クォーター」、decade（10年）「デケイド」

Unit 23 Marketing

Warm-up

Check 1 Match the words to the definitions. Write the letters on the lines.

1. launch   _____   a. study of consumers' needs and preferences
2. market research _____   b. buying and selling online
3. e-commerce   _____   c. special symbol used to represent a company or product
4. trademark   _____   d. creation and maintenance of a good product or
5. public relations _____   company image
                            e. to introduce a new product

Check 2 Choose the correct word from the box to complete each sentence.

| create | demand | directly | factors | success |

1. There are the four basic (   ) of marketing: product, price, place, and promotion.

2. Marketing plays an important part in the (   ) of a new product.

3. The company mailed marketing letters (   ) to customers.

4. The company has started an advertising campaign to (   ) a favorable brand image.

5. Market research shows that there is real (   ) for a new type of carry-on suitcase.

Test Questions

Part 1 Photographs   90

1.   2.

    Ⓐ Ⓑ Ⓒ Ⓓ   Ⓐ Ⓑ Ⓒ Ⓓ

52

Part 2 Question-Response 🔊 91

3. Mark your answer. Ⓐ Ⓑ Ⓒ
4. Mark your answer. Ⓐ Ⓑ Ⓒ

Part 3 Short Conversations 🔊 92

5. Why does the man say TV sales have declined?
   (A) The workers are inexperienced.   (B) The sales department is short-handed.
   (C) The economy is in poor condition.   (D) Production is behind.

6. When will the woman take action against the problem?
   (A) Now   (B) Tomorrow
   (C) The day after tomorrow   (D) When they send a report

7. How are they going to try to fix the problem?
   (A) By increasing the number of workers
   (B) By working overtime
   (C) By changing the sales strategy
   (D) By hiring more aggressive workers

Part 4 Short Talks 🔊 93

8. What has happened to the TV sales figures?
   (A) Sales are booming.
   (B) The decline in sales has been stopped for now.
   (C) The crisis is continuing.
   (D) Sales are still falling.

9. How can the company increase contact with customers?
   (A) Use email   (B) Increase the number of sales personnel
   (C) Start work earlier   (D) Change the schedule

10. What does the speaker recommend?
    (A) Cut down on staff
    (B) More overtime
    (C) Increase staff
    (D) Change the sales areas the staff are responsible for

Follow-up

> **集中力の持続**
>
> - リスニング問題では音声が流れていて待ってくれませんから、聞き取れない問題に引きずられないで、気持ちを切り替えて次の問題に集中しましょう。
> - 時間が足りないと感じる人は、時間を作る工夫をしましょう。Part 3 や Part 4 では設問の先読みが大切です。会話やトークが流れた後に設問が読まれますが、会話やトークが終わったらすぐに答えをマークして、設問が読まれている間に次の会話の設問に目を通すのがリスニング攻略のコツです。リスニングの45分間、集中力を持続できるように日頃からトレーニングしておきましょう。

Unit 24 Mini Test 4

Part 1 Photographs   94

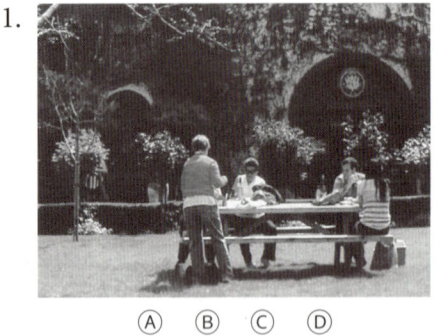

1. Ⓐ Ⓑ Ⓒ Ⓓ

2. Ⓐ Ⓑ Ⓒ Ⓓ

3. Ⓐ Ⓑ Ⓒ Ⓓ

4. Ⓐ Ⓑ Ⓒ Ⓓ

Part 2 Question-Response   95

5. Mark your answer.   Ⓐ Ⓑ Ⓒ

6. Mark your answer.   Ⓐ Ⓑ Ⓒ

7. Mark your answer.   Ⓐ Ⓑ Ⓒ

8. Mark your answer.   Ⓐ Ⓑ Ⓒ

9. Mark your answer.   Ⓐ Ⓑ Ⓒ

Part 3 Short Conversations   96

10. What is the news about the foreign company?
    (A) It has already made a big profit.
    (B) Its product will be in stores next month.
    (C) It has changed its policy.
    (D) It has made a similar product.

11. What will the new sales strategy emphasize?
    (A) How cheap the company's brushes are
    (B) That the copy is an improvement on the original item
    (C) That the company's brushes are more reliable
    (D) Product safety

12. What will they do if the new strategy doesn't work?
    (A) Consult someone at a law office
    (B) Cut prices and start a price war
    (C) Make an agreement with the foreign company
    (D) Redesign the packaging

Part 4 Short Talks   97

13. What does the speaker say is wrong with the customer service section?
    (A) The staff has been working too hard.
    (B) Its image is not what it should be.
    (C) It lacks sufficient personnel.
    (D) It has lost most of the company's regular customers.

14. What does the speaker say the Call Center needs to do?
    (A) Be more honest with customers
    (B) Make empty promises
    (C) Trust the customer's judgement
    (D) Act happy

15. What should the staff do if a client can't make up his or her mind?
    (A) Ask the client to call the Call Center again the next week
    (B) Become more aggressive
    (C) Call the client back in two or three days
    (D) Tell him or her about the company's excellent corporate image and unequaled reputation

Listening Breakthrough for the TOEIC® Test

著作権法上、無断複写・複製は禁じられています。

Listening Breakthrough for the TOEIC® Test　　[B-769]
TOEIC® テストのリスニング攻略

1 刷	2015年1月15日
5 刷	2022年8月26日

著 者	テリー・オブライエン	Terry O'Brien
	三原　京	Kei Mihara
	秀野　作次郎	Sakujiro Shuno
	木村　博是	Hiroshi Kimura

発行者　南雲　一範　　Kazunori Nagumo
発行所　株式会社　南雲堂
　　　　〒162-0801　東京都新宿区山吹町361
　　　　NAN'UN-DO Co., Ltd.
　　　　361 Yamabuki-cho, Shinjuku-ku, Tokyo 162-0801, Japan
　　　　振替口座：00160-0-46863
　　　　TEL: 03-3268-2311(代表)／FAX: 03-3269-2486

編 集	加藤　敦
製 版	木内　早苗
装 丁	Nスタジオ
検 印	省　略
コード	ISBN 978-4-523-17769-2　C0082

Printed in Japan

E-mail　nanundo@post.email.ne.jp
URL　　https://www.nanun-do.co.jp/

南雲堂の英語書

リスニング + リーディングに頻出
音で聞いて、目で見て、
ズバリ対応！

本書の特徴

▶ 精選された TOEID® テスト頻出単語とイディオム
▶ レベル別とテーマ別に分類
▶ 必須単語を例文の中で確認し、覚えることができる
▶ 赤チェックシート学習
▶ 文法の弱点補強ができる
▶ CD 音声でリスニングの訓練ができる

新 TOEIC® テストズバリ出る英単語ファイル
赤チェックシート付

三原　京著

A5判　295ページ CD2枚付　定価(本体 2,000円+税)
ISBN978-4-523-26482-8

南雲堂
NAN'UN-DO

南雲堂のTOEIC対策本！
トントン拍子でスコア・アップ！夢をかなえる学習法！

ネコの『トントン』

英語の師匠 オーガ＆セイン プレゼンツ
TOEIC® テスト攻略 トントンメソッド

- **特長1** コロコロ覚えるTOEIC頻出英単語！
- **特長2** ドンドン読めるスピード・リーディング！
- **特長3** グングンわかるシャドーイング！

デイビッド・セイン

大賀リヱ

◎ 銅メダルコース ＜Book 1＞
　　TOEIC 400点〜600点レベル（154ページ）

◎ 銅メダルコース ＜Book 2＞
　　TOEIC 500点〜700点レベル（154ページ）

◎ 銀メダルコース
　　TOEIC 600点〜800点レベル（160ページ）

◎ 金メダルコース
　　TOEIC 700点〜（180ページ）

大賀リヱ・デイビッド・セイン著／46判　定価（各本体1000円＋税）

▶ 南雲堂
英語語学書最新刊!!

やっぱり、やっぱり英文法!!
英文法をやさしく学ぶ1ヵ月イメージトレーニングメソッド

イラスト＋写真で
1ヵ月スピードマスター **英文法『イメトレ』**

アンドルー・ベネット 著
小宮 徹

A5判（166ページ）
定価（本体1,400円＋税）

MP3 CD付

比較
The car is **faster than** the motorcycle.

副詞節
She talks on the phone **before she rides her bike**.

be動詞
She **is** surprised.

条件節
If the sign **falls**, the boy **may be** hurt.

未来
The race **will be** very close.

副詞
The dog is **extremely** large.

「言葉」ではなく「イメージ」で学ぶ英文法
これ1冊で中学〜高校で学習する英文法を完全理解
高校までに学習した英語の総おさらいが可能

南雲堂　〒162-0801
東京都新宿区山吹町361
TEL 03-3268-2384　FAX 03-3260-5425